PLANTS AT YOUR FINGERTIPS

PLANTS FOR THE
WILDLIFE
GARDEN

PETER THURMAN

First published in Great Britain in 1994 by
PAVILION BOOKS LIMITED
26 Upper Ground, London SE1 9PD

Text © Peter Thurman 1994

Conceived, edited and designed by Russell Ash & Bernard Higton
Picture research by Julia Pashley
Plant consultant Tony Lord

The moral right of the author has been asserted.

A CIP catalogue record for this book is available from the
British Library.

ISBN 1 85793 107 6

Printed and bound in Singapore by Tien Wah Press

2 4 6 8 10 9 7 5 3 1

This book may be ordered by post direct from the publisher.
Please contact the Marketing Department.
But try your bookshop first.

CONTENTS

INTRODUCTION

WHY CREATE A WILDLIFE GARDEN?

Quite simply, wild plants and animals give people plea-sure. They inspire writers, artists and musicians or provide the means for hobbies such as fishing, walking and bird watching which rely on wildlife and the countryside. In the garden something is going on throughout the year to fascinate and absorb. There is nothing more satisfying than your first glimpse of a nuthatch feeding from a string of nuts, or dragonflies hovering over your very own pond. Watching wildlife on your own doorstep is both interesting and educational.

For quite selfish reasons we should consider wildlife as a resource. Very many plants and animals are of great value to us as food, or as raw material for drugs and other commer-cial materials. New uses are discovered every week. Wildlife can be looked upon as a massive pool of genes which has only partially been exploited. By conserving wildlife, we are retaining the widest possible choice of options for the future. Once a species becomes extinct, it is lost forever.

And that's the trouble: plants and animals *are* becoming extinct. Only a hundred years ago a walk in a woodland or down a leafy lane would have been rewarded with the sight of scores of different species of butterflies, for example. Today many species are in decline. Modern farming and

OPPOSITE: SMALL TORTOISESHELL BUTTERFLIES ON STONECROP.

forestry methods, in particular the widespread use of chemicals, the removal of hedgerows and the draining of wetlands has led to dwindling numbers of our native flowers, animals and insects. A lowland woodland can contain up to 5,000 species of plants and animals, and in prehistoric times most of the low areas of Britain were covered by trees; today only nine per cent of Britain is tree covered.

The beautiful Adonis blue butterfly is rarely seen on the chalky downlands where it was once abundant and the marsh fritillary, which used to add its orange and brown hues to colourful grasses and flowers in marshy meadows, is now very scarce. In 1981 the Nature Conservancy Council (now English Nature) estimated a 60 to 70 per cent loss of the species caused by the draining of wet meadows so that it has now almost vanished from eastern England and the Midlands.

Modern needs for housing, supermarkets, offices, factories and roads encroach on wildlife space, displacing the flora and fauna which sometimes require very specific habitats for survival. Unfortunately, the needs of the former residents often come low on the list of priorities when a new development is under way – even if the land sustains unique native species.

Yet even a small corner of a garden can help to redress the balance by recreating the kinds of habitats we are increasingly removing from the countryside. A tiny patch within a city garden – even one surrounded by urban mayhem – can provide a safe haven for an enormous range of animal, insect and plant life if allowed to be a little on the 'wild side'.

A wildlife garden does not have to

be a weed-ridden wilderness and it should certainly not be left to chance. Creating a wildlife garden does not mean leaving it to go wild – quite the reverse. Careful planning and the right choice of plants are essential to ensure that your wildlife area and the community of creatures that live within it thrive and enhance the pleasure derived from your garden.

A garden full of wildlife is well-balanced and healthy. Many of the animals you attract will pay you 'rent' by keeping the population of garden pests in check and by pollinating flowering and fruiting plants.

Some features in a wildlife garden have the added bonus of being both cheap and easy to maintain. To a degree, a wild garden or feature looks after itself. This is partly to do with the wildlife 'style' and your attitude of mind. In a wildlife border, shrubs can be left unpruned, it does not matter if they spread into their neighbours. This can not only look attractive but it will also provide more shelter and protection and even more flowers. In a wildlife garden daisies and dandelions can be left on a lawn – and in fact positively encouraged by fewer mowings.

What would a garden be without the sounds of wildlife? Birdsong, buzzing bees and grasshoppers chattering provide a background symphony we barely notice, but would miss dreadfully if it suddenly stopped. Today, sadly, the most important reason to consider a wildlife garden, or section of a garden, is the simple need for us all to help conserve our natural heritage.

Wildlife gardens are not an entirely modern concept. Some 18th-century landscape gardeners such as Richard Payne Knight rebelled against the smooth, civilized 'parkscapes' made famous by Capability Brown and created wilder features such as gorges and dense woodlands where dead trees were left where they had fallen to provide a home from home for insects, mammals and birds. They perhaps did not realize the bonus for wildlife from their efforts to create an aesthetic wilderness but, nevertheless, many species reaped the benefits. In the next century, two famous gardeners, William Robinson and Gertrude Jekyll, encouraged a move away from the formal Victorian style of gardening and promoted wild flower meadows, natural water features and woodland gardens.

MAKING A WILDLIFE GARDEN

The basic requirement when planning a wildlife garden is to provide adequate food and shelter for our native fauna. Do not be put off if you have only a tiny plot. It is possible to convert even the smallest garden into a haven for wildlife. Food for animals will be supplied mainly by plants – seeds, fruits or the nectar from flowers for example. So correct plant selection is vital. Sheltered living quarters and a source of food can be provided by a wide range of features, many of which, such as a flower border, are attractive in their own right.

The idea is to mimic nature, albeit on a smaller scale, by creating various habitats. Even very small gardens have room for a bird-table, bat box, a patch of wild flowers or a mini-pond. And that's all it takes.

INGREDIENTS FOR A WILDLIFE GARDEN

Here are some ideas for features and mini-habitats that will attract animals into your garden.

Hedges, thickets and screens
Any dense planting, such as a boundary hedge (far more attractive than a fence) or windbreak will provide cover, food and a suitable nesting site for many birds. Native plants, in particular, provide natural food and shelter for

STARLING FEEDING ON ROWAN BERRIES

wildlife. Plants such as hawthorn, field maple, hornbeam, holly and beech are among the best from the point of view of the animals who will live in them and for the people who look at them, as they are all attractive and provide a wonderful backdrop to the rest of the garden. Some exotic conifers with their dense evergreen canopies provide especially sheltered homes preferred by some species of birds, such as wrens.

Food plants and wild flower borders, meadows or lawns
Picture a sweep of shrubs and perennial flowers all carefully selected to provide a refuelling station for wildlife – seemingly alive with butterflies, bees and other insects visiting the blooms for nectar. The massed humming chorus and frantic activity is exciting to watch and to hear. In autumn these same shrubs can provide seeds and berries for birds.

Making a border or bed of wildlife-attracting shrubs and flowers is easy, it is just a matter of appropriate plant selection, depending on what types of animals and insects you want to see and encourage.

In a very small garden, just a single climbing honeysuckle over the porch and other perennial evening-scented plants will attract moths.

All or part of even a small lawn can be turned into a miniature meadow – simply halt the mowing ritual and stop spraying with weed killer. Access or circulatory paths are easily obtained by continuing to cut just where these are required. A floristic meadow or lawn is a little more complicated than a border but well within the bounds of every gardener's ability. The combination of grasses and wild flowers can be a stunning garden feature and also a home and food source to many hundreds of insects. These in turn attract insect-eating birds. Excellent results can be achieved by sowing wild flower seeds, now available in mixtures suitable for most soils and sites, some with suitable grasses, or, more expensively, by planting 'plugs' of commercially available wild flowers.

Consistent management is the key to a successful flower meadow or lawn. The area needs to be cut after but not before the flowers have set seed. Large areas will require some sort of machinery to make the cut, but a small area could be strimmed or scythed. These mowings should always be removed. A second light cut may be needed, timed according to the flowering season of the plants.

As an alternative, another type of management will form a low level meadow that is cut throughout the growing season to keep a sward at about three to four inches. A different floral-grass mix will develop, but this area can be managed with normal adjustable rotary mowers and does not demand specialized harvesting equipment.

To create a new wild flower and grass area the most important factor is the nutrient status of the soil. The poorer the soil, the better it is for wild flowers. This means that a wild flower feature in your garden can be started where that old heap of hard-core was left or where the builders never put back the top-soil. Food plant and wild flower areas can be created in any environment and any soil type. It is just a matter of selecting the right plants for each situation – and that is easy because for every wild feature in your garden there is a wild plant that grows in that situation naturally. This is another important advantage of a wildlife garden. It is all about working *with* the site conditions that already exist and not fighting against them. Some of the best wildlife gardens are

A WILD FLOWER MEADOW AT THE HEIGHT OF SUMMER.

based on this single basic principle – usually because they have been developed on sites that have a naturally dominating and unifying character or habitat type such as heathland, chalk-pit or stream-side. Wildlife gardening exploits what you already have and avoids anything too alien or unnatural.

Very few people have a garden big enough to include a woodland, but just one tree – perhaps a small native, such as hazel or a berrying species such as mountain ash – will create a woodland effect or woodland edge beneath its crown. Underplanting with low-growing shade-tolerant plants will increase the cover for wildlife as well as improving the overall appearance. Foxgloves, primroses, bluebells, violets and honeysuckle are all woodland, field-layer plants that need and appreciate the shade and shelter provided by the trees above. For gardeners with 0.25 hectares/0.6 acres or more of land available to be planted with broad-leaf trees, there are grants available from the Forestry Authority (formerly the Forestry Commission) to assist.

A WETLAND PASTURE AND WILDLIFE POND

PONDS AND WET AREAS

A natural pond or area of boggy ground makes a fascinating wildlife habitat. It is a seething soap opera of life and death, killing or being killed, sex and the day to day life of thousands of creatures.

A pond will attract frogs, newts and dragonflies as well as birds to drink. The pond should be positioned well away from trees, preferably in full sun with plants and/or a rockery next to at least one bank to provide cover for young reptiles and shade and protection for hibernating amphibians. Frogs are a gardener's friend. They eat slugs, which can reach plague proportions and destroy large clumps of succulent foliage in one evening – especially hostas and delphiniums. The only way to keep frogs in your garden is to provide them with a pond.

A wildlife pond should have sloping edges and shallow

areas. This enables birds to drink and bathe, amphibians safely to spawn and hedgehogs and other mammals to escape if they are unlucky enough to fall in. Shallow or boggy areas will also allow you to grow marginal plants that will create yet another habitat type. Although the shallow areas are important, some areas should be over 60 cm deep so that they don't freeze solid in a hard winter. A paved area to one side of the pond allows easy access and viewing. Slabs overlapping the pond edge provide amphibians with shade and somewhere to hide from birds and cats.

Different pond sizes will attract different wildlife. Generally the larger the better, but some dragonflies for example, will breed in ponds with a surface area as small as four square metres. Toads and great crested newts prefer larger ponds (15 square metres or more). Frogs like to spawn in water 7-10 cm deep, amongst submerged aquatic plants, while toads and newts spawn in water between 10 and 50 cm deep.

A pond contains an enormous amount of living organisms, many of them invisible to the naked eye but all an essential part of the balanced eco-system. Insects such as dragonflies, damselflies, bugs, beetles including the amusing water-boatmen *are* clearly visible

A FROG BASKS IN THE SHALLOWS OF A WILDLIFE POND

and their dramatic lives are a great 'crowd puller'.

So how do you make a wildlife pond? Don't automatically choose a wet or damp hollow that may already be important to wildlife. In a nutshell, dig a hole and then use a material to keep the water in. Polythene or butyl rubber liners are simple and relatively cheap. Line the hole with sand, old newspapers or carpet to prevent puncturing, position the liner and fill with water. The liner should obviously be bigger than the pond. The edges are then buried or tucked into the soil or covered with turf. Add a further layer of sand or soil over the liner once you have laid it to reduce the breaking down effect of sunlight and to create a more natural 'living' layer at the bottom of the pond.

Other methods include the use of pre-formed plastic liners. They come in all shapes and sizes but are best used for formal water features. They can be difficult to fit and level and are usually steep-sided. If you have a heavy clay soil, a wildlife pond can be formed by smearing or puddling the clay to create a seal – but it may leak at a later date, especially in times of drought. Concrete ponds take time and skill to construct and generally have a sterile, unnatural appearance.

Having filled your pond with water, allow it to stand for three or four days before planting. This allows the chlorine in tap water to dissipate. Better still, allow your wildlife pond to stock itself. You will be surprised how quickly it is colonized by insects, frogs and plants. A bucket of water from an established pond will speed the process up.

The secret is to create an ecologically balanced habitat. For this, a wildlife pond should include submerged, floating and marginal or waters-edge plants. These will seed themselves eventually, or you can buy growing plants from retail outlets. The submerged types should include species that oxygenate the water, such as *Ceratophyllum* (hornwort) and *Myriophyllum* (water milfoil).

Fish eat tadpoles, but sticklebacks and minnows will provide interest without reducing the population too drastically. Don't be afraid if your pond dries up or the water level gets low occasionally – some fish will die and address any imbalance in the wildlife community. Ornamental fish such as koi are not wholly appropriate in a wildlife pond. Beware of transferring spawn or adult frogs or toads between ponds because you may be spreading disease and it

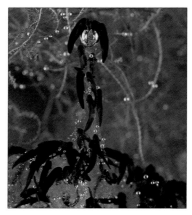

TADPOLES SHORTLY AFTER HATCHING

is illegal to move great crested newts or natterjack toads without a license.

In winter, always try to keep a hole in the ice so that birds can wash and drink. It also prevents concrete or rigid liners from being damaged by the expanding ice. A tub of hot water placed in the ice will melt a hole.

If a pond is out of the question, a miniature wildlife pond can be created in a half oak barrel or ceramic sink. Bury it in the ground, use stones to create a slope on one side and plant the other with marginal plants.

A word of warning: many children drown every year in even the shallowest of ponds. Toddlers and ponds of any sort just do not go together. Total and complete access must be denied at all times to children except when constantly supervised. If there is any doubt, it is not worth the risk. Create your wildlife pond at a later date when any children who are likely to visit your garden are older and fully aware of the danger.

SOME OTHER FEATURES

• Bird tables and nut baskets will attract a great number of birds to your garden. Watching them feed will give hours of pleasure.

• Piles of logs, leaves, rubble or rocks provide ideal homes for small mammals, especially hedgehogs, and mini-habitats for many other animals and insects.

• A compost heap not only recycles garden waste but can provide a breeding ground for slug-eating slow worms and also attract insect eating birds.

Let's look more closely at some of the wildlife we wish to attract:

Birds
A garden without the sound and sight of birds is incomplete. Many are also great allies of gardeners. Underground lawn pests such as leatherjackets and cutworms will be eaten by starlings and ants will be sought out by green woodpeckers.

Providing food will greatly increase the range of birds that visit your garden. While tits are waiting their turn on the nut basket, they will feed on aphids and other insect eggs. Shrubs that produce berries in the autumn, such as *Berberis*, *Pyracantha*, *Cotoneaster* and many British native shrubs will be a big attraction for a large number of birds stocking up fat reserves for the winter ahead. Wild annual and perennial flowers such as sunflowers, Michaelmas daisies and golden-rod supply seeds for gold and green finches. Bullfinches prefer wallflowers and snapdragons.

British native trees and shrubs tend not to suffer from serious pests and diseases and they are often hosts to a wide range of insects that are food to insect-eating birds. Several natives make good hedging plants (beech, yew and hawthorn for example). This allows even the smallest of gardens to grow a wide range of attractive plants without taking up too much precious space. Regular clipping not only controls the size of the hedge, it also induces denser growth, making it ideal for nesting birds.

Nest boxes will ensure the long-term presence of birds in your garden. There may be plenty of food for birds but nowhere for them to nest unless boxes are put up. Blue and great tits especially, but over 60 species altogether are known to use nest boxes – these include tawny owls, spotted flycatchers and even kestrels.

Butterflies
Butterflies will visit your garden if you simply provide warm shelter and nectar – you do not have to live in the country or turn your garden into a neglected jungle. They are cold-blooded and require warmth before they become active. Once mobile, they will search for a warm sheltered spot to bask in the sun's rays and then find a source of nectar. Nectar-rich flowers in a cold shady position will be ignored.

Getting butterflies to breed in your garden may be a little more difficult for many species, but a wild patch of weeds such as nettles is all they require to encourage breeding activity. The only serious caterpillar pests are the large and small whites which feed voraciously on cabbages. But in a well-balanced wildlife garden there should be plenty of predators to keep them under control. Many butterflies have definite preferences for nectar from specific flowers, but most will drink from a variety of plants.

Butterflies are active from spring to autumn, so plant a good range of varieties with different flowering times to sustain them throughout this period. Late summer is the peak time for butterfly activity, so plants that flower then should take precedence. Plant in bold clumps so that you get a mass of flowers which flash a large 'neon' sign to advertise their presence to butterflies. Native species, such as small tortoise-shells and the peacock that overwinter as butterflies, appear on the first warm days of spring. Others overwinter as caterpillars or pupae (for example wall browns and small copper) or are immigrants like the painted lady and appear later in May and June. The butterfly population then builds up over the summer months.

Butterflies generally favour the more common garden plants or even straight species, rather than the highly bred cultivated varieties. Old fashioned types of cottage garden flowers such as candytuft, sweet William, lavender and hyssop are all attractive to butterflies. Butterflies, together with bees are the main instigators of pollination in the garden and are therefore important for good crops of fruit.

Other animals and insects
Many other animals and insects are also positively beneficial to the garden. Hedgehogs, for example, eat slugs, grubs and a number of other pests. To attract them, create areas where they can hibernate in winter, such as log piles. Feed in autumn with bread and milk diluted 50:50 with water.

OPPOSITE: A LONG-EARED BAT AT DUSK.

Many wildlife gardeners attract larger mammals such as badgers and foxes by providing tempting foods on a regular basis. Hours of enjoyment are to be had watching these shy visitors at night. To many people squirrels are a pest but their antics can be great fun to watch and they will visit a garden given very little excuse.

All British bats eat large numbers of insects, including pests such as aphids, mosquitoes, crane flies and moths. It is difficult to encourage them unless they are already in the neighbourhood but, if they are known to visit your garden, you can try to encourage them to roost or hibernate. Bats like to roost in warm places during the day and hibernate somewhere cool during winter. Carefully positioned bat boxes should fulfil both these functions.

Small mammals such as mice and voles also eat garden pests. They will be attracted to sheltered areas and long grass.

Many insects are also pest predators or parasites (they lay their eggs in or on a pest, which then feed on the host when they hatch). Mankind has successfully harnessed this phenomenon in certain cases and some are now commercially available under the term 'biological control'. Ladybirds, ground and rove beetles, centipedes, lacewings, hoverflies and parasitic wasps are all beneficial insects performing this role naturally in your garden. Dispensing with chemical sprays or using them extremely sparingly will prevent harming beneficial insects and keep population levels up. Plenty of sheltered areas, ground cover and nectar-producing flowers will all help encourage these insects into your garden.

Do keep at least one small area of your garden totally wild – which will be a haven in every sense of the word to a wide range of animals. In particular, try to find a place for a clump of stinging nettles. It is a food plant to a very large number of butterfly larvae including red admiral, comma, peacock and small tortoiseshell – and home to many other insects.

PLANTS DIRECTORY

The following plants all play various roles in
a wildlife garden. There is something for
every type of wildlife garden, from a small
back yard to a garden of some acres.

Plants are listed in alphabetical order of Latin name
followed by the common name, if any. The common name is
excluded if it is identical to the Latin name.

The 'fact line' shows, in order:
Size – average height in metres and spread in metres of a
mature plant
Soil – tolerances, preferences or special requirements
Site – tolerances, preferences or special requirements

ALYSSUM SAXATILE (syn. *Aurinia saxatilis*)

A common, easy to grow evergreen perennial, rockery or border edging plant. The masses of small yellow flowers are produced from April to June over grey foliage. Visited for the flower nectar by butterflies, bees and predators such as hover-flies and wasps. There are many improved forms available. The annual varieties of alyssum will perform the same function in the summer.

0.2 × 0.4   Poor, well-drained soils   Open sunny site

ARABIS ROCK CRESS

Semi-evergreen perennial carpeter, for growing over low walls, in rock gardens or on the edges of paths. Flowers appear in March–April and sporadically beyond into summer. There are a number of species but *A. caucasica* is the most popular. It has white flowers but there are pink and red flow-ered forms. Orange tip butterfly larvae will feed on the leaves of this plant as well as on lady's smock and honesty.

0.2 × 0.6   Well-drained   Sun or part shade

ASTER MICHAELMAS DAISY

A large, famous group of decorative herbaceous perennials coming in a wide range of heights and flower colours (white, pink, lavender, red and blue). They produce their daisy flow-ers mainly in late summer and on into autumn. Although not very wild looking, they are invaluable in a wildlife garden. The flowers are visited by butterflies, such as peacock and comma and other insects for nectar. In the autumn the seeds are eaten by birds.

0.3 to 1.2 × 0.4 to 0.8   Any well-drained soil   Full sun is preferred

AUBRIETA

Another reliable low-spreading perennial with a large range of flower colour forms (blues, reds, mauves and pinks), ideal for containers, raised beds or the front of a border. The flowers,

Alyssum saxatile

Arabis caucasica

Aster amellus 'King George'

Aubrieta

Berberis darwinii

Calendula officinalis

Buddleja davidii var. *nanhoensis* 'Nanho Blue'

Calluna vulgaris 'H.E. Beale'

which bloom in late spring and early summer, are a good nectar source for insects, especially bumble bees. A number of butterflies, such as the brimstone, painted lady, red admiral and small tortoiseshell are attracted to the flowers.

0.1 × 0.60   Well-drained, preferably limy soil   Open sunny site

BERBERIS BARBERRY

A large genus of deciduous and evergreen shrubs that includes both dwarfs and giants, all of which are spiny. The orange or yellow flowers appear in April and May with black, purple or red berries in autumn. In a wildlife garden they have many uses: some species, such as *B. × stenophylla*, make excellent dense hedges, providing shelter and nesting sites for birds. The berries are also much loved by birds.

0.4 to 3.0 × 0.4 to 2.0   Any soil type   Sun or part shade

BUDDLEJA DAVIDII BUTTERFLY OR BOMBSITE BUSH

A deciduous shrub renowned for being able to grow almost anywhere, including amongst rubble – hence one of its common names. In mid-summer the highly scented flower spikes attract many butterflies, especially tortoiseshells, peacocks and red admirals, as well as other insects. There are many named varieties differing principally in flower colour (white, lilac, deep purple, blue and pink). This is probably the number one shrub for butterflies. Other species of *Buddleja* are almost as good, some, such as *B. alternifolia*, flowering earlier.

3.0 × 2.5   Any well-drained soil   Open, exposed site

CALENDULA OFFICINALIS POT MARIGOLD

An old cottage garden hardy annual with flat orange flowers, now often superseded by the many cultivated forms. Excellent for patio tubs or as fillers in a raised border. The flowers are visited by many insects, especially the comma, red admiral and small tortoiseshell butterflies, as well as some moths at night.

0.5 × 0.3   Especially good in poor soils   Sun or part shade

Caryopteris × clandonensis

CALLUNA VULGARIS HEATHER OR LING

The familiar native evergreen ground-cover of mountain, moorland and heath land. There are hundreds of varieties, all flowering in late summer and usually into autumn and often combined with conifers to produce a distinct and low–maintenance style of garden. For the best effect plant in bold drifts, but they are also ideal for rock outcrops and even containers. The dense low habit is home to many insects, spiders and small mammals and the flowers are much loved by butterflies and bees.

0.2 × 0.4 Well-drained, hungry acid soil Full sun

CARYOPTERIS × CLANDONENSIS SHRUBBY VERBENA

A most attractive blue flowered and grey foliaged deciduous shrub. Perfect for a shrub border or amongst herbaceous perennials and roses. The flowers appear in late summer and are visited by a wide range of insects.

0.5 × 0.5 Well-drained, including chalk Sun

Ceanothus thyrsiflorus var. *repens*

CEANOTHUS CALIFORNIAN LILAC
Evergreen or deciduous wall shrubs requiring a sheltered, frost-free position. Most varieties have brilliant blue flowers in dense clusters in spring or early autumn. The dense branching on a warm wall makes it an ideal nesting site for small birds and, when in flower, the whole plant is alive with bees and other insects.

2.0 to 4.0 × 2.0 to 3.0   Well-drained loam   South facing wall

CENTRANTHUS RUBER RED VALERIAN
A tough herbaceous perennial with fleshy glaucous leaves and large long heads of minute deep pink flowers in summer. It often seeds itself, especially on limestone walls or stony banks. Butterflies such as the small tortoiseshell visit the flowers during the day and moths such as the elephant hawk moth at night .

0.9 × 0.9   Any soil, including shallow chalk   Open exposed and coastal sites

CHAMAECYPARIS LAWSONIANA LAWSON CYPRESS

An evergreen conifer available in all shapes, sizes and foliage colours. The dwarf forms are suitable for containers or rock gardens. The larger types make excellent hedges and screens – and this is their main role in a wildlife garden. Birds such as the greenfinch love to nest in the congested branch system and a border of nectar-rich flowers will benefit from the shelter they can provide as a hedge. Less vigorous and more manageable than Leyland cypress.

1.0 to 5.0 × 0.5 to 2.0   Moist, but well-drained   Open but sheltered

CISTUS SUN ROSE

Small Mediterranean shrubs for dry banks and open positions. The flowers, which are especially loved by bees, are very freely produced in early summer and are mainly white, although on some species they are pink or purple. Many have attractive, greyish hairy or succulent leaves that exude a sweet-smelling gum.

1.0 × 1.0   Free draining, dry soils including chalk   Exposed full sun; avoid frost pockets

CORNUS ALBA RED-BARKED DOGWOOD

Attractive shrubs producing a thicket of stems. There are forms with different coloured stems and leaf variegations. Our native species is *C. sanguinea* and both are ideal for hedges, thickets and wildlife cover. The inconspicuous flowers bloom in early summer and are visited by butterflies. The black berries of *C. sanguinea* are eaten by birds in autumn. Effective in a wildlife border, or, as they tolerate wet conditions, for the edges of larger ponds.

1.5 × 1.5   Wet or dry soils   Sun or part shade

CORYLUS AVELLANA COMMON HAZEL

Our native hazel is usually grown as a shrub or small tree, or can be regularly cut down hard (coppicing) to maintain its

Centranthus ruber

Cistus

Corylus avellana

Chamaecyparis lawsoniana
'Elegantissima'

Cotoneaster frigidus

Dianthus barbatus

allotted space in a small garden. The yellow catkin flowers appear in February. Useful for hedging, screening and providing shelter and shade. It is home to many insects, birds will nest in densely branched specimens and birds and mammals will eat its nuts in winter.

2.0 to 5.0 × 3.0 Any soil Cold exposed sites, sun or shade

COTONEASTER
An important genus of decorative, deciduous and evergreen shrubs or small trees. Their main ornamental attribute is the red or occasionally yellow berries in autumn which are thoroughly enjoyed by birds. Some varieties such as *C. frigidus* make fine hedges which are suitable for nesting.

0.5 to 5.0 × 0.5 to 3.0 Any soil Sun or shade

CRATAEGUS MONOGYNA MAY, HAWTHORN OR QUICK
A familiar small native tree or hedgerow plant. White flowers in May are followed by red fruits (haws) in autumn. Plant as an informal hedge, clipped after the berries have been eaten

by birds or as a small specimen tree that will provide a wood-land edge habitat beneath. Either way, birds will also nest amongst the branches – for example songthrush and chaffinch. Home to many species of insects and caterpillars.

2.0 to 6.0 × 1.0 to 4.0   Any soil   Sun or part shade

DIANTHUS BARBATUS SWEET WILLIAM

A much loved hardy biennial of British gardens bearing dense, flattened heads of red or red and white flowers in mid-summer. Hoverflies, wasps, bees and butterflies such as the meadow brown will all visit the flowers.

0.35 × 0.2   Well-drained, non-acidic   Full sun

ERICA CARNEA HEATHER

Dwarf evergreen hummock-forming shrub. With *Calluna vulgaris*, this is the most commonly planted species of heather with the added bonus of being chalk-tolerant. Like *Calluna*, it has hundreds of named varieties with miniature bell-like flowers of white, pink or purple that appear between November and April. The dense habitat provides cover for many animals and insects. On warm days in late autumn or early spring the flowers are sought out by many grateful insects.

0.2 × 0.4   Well-drained soil including chalk   Full sun

ERYSIMUM CHEIRI (syn. *Cheiranthus cheiri*)
WALLFLOWER

This hardy biennial, along with tulips, forget-me-nots and primroses are planted in their millions every year for spring colour. Flower colour ranges from yellow to red. The Siberian wallflower (*E. allionii*) is yellow or orange and dwarf. Both are easy to grow from seed and ideal for containers or en masse in their own bed. The deliciously scented flowers are a real pull for insects, especially butterflies. If allowed to set seed, birds will have a feed too.

0.3 × 0.3   Any soil, especially chalky   Full sun

ESCALLONIA

Dense evergreen shrubs for milder areas, bearing clusters of small white, pink or red flowers from June and on into autumn. They make excellent hedges, especially in coastal regions, which are perfect for nesting purposes. All are visited by insects when in flower. *E. rubra* var. *macrantha* seems to be especially popular with nectar seekers.

2.0 × 1.5   Any well-drained soil   Sun or sheltered partial shade

FILIPENDULA ULMARIA   MEADOWSWEET

A tall native perennial ideal for the edges of a wildlife pond or wet grassy and shady areas. The creamy-white flower umbels are in bloom from June to September and fill the air with a sweet, memorable scent. The seeds are eaten by birds. This is one of the many beautiful wild flowers with which our countryside is blessed that is now readily available as commercially produced seed.

1.0 × 0.5   Moist soil   Partial shade

HEBE   SHRUBBY VERONICA

Evergreen, slightly tender shrubs ranging greatly in size from compact hummocks to large shrubs. They vary greatly in leaf and flower, but their appeal in a wildlife garden is that they all tend to flower for a long time (June into autumn). Many insects, but especially bees and bumblebees, love the nectar. *H. albicans* and *H. salicifolia* are among the best and the toughest.

0.5 to 3.0 × 0.5 to 2.0   Well-drained   Sheltered sun or light shade

HEDERA HELIX   COMMON IVY

Our native evergreen climber or sprawler is a must for the wildlife garden. It will grow anywhere – up and over walls, in hedges and trees or as a ground carpeter. The adult form, normally seen only on mature specimens that have scrambled up some form of support, flower and fruit profusely. Ivy

Erysimum cheiri

Escallonia

Hebe salcifolia

Filipendula ulmaria

Hedera helix

provides cover and hibernation sites for many insects, which in turn attract birds and encourage them to nest. When in flower, ivy is swarming with insects, especially bees. The purplish-black berries are also eaten by birds. A really useful plant in the wildlife garden.

6.0 × 3.0   Any soil   Sun or shade

HESPERIS MATRONALIS DAME'S VIOLET
An erect perennial plant naturalized in hedgerows and on banks or road verges with fragrant white or purple summer flowers in broad panicles. Caterpillars such as the green-veined white and orange tip feed on it. Moths are attracted to the flowers at night and a wide range of insects during the day.

0.8 × 0.4   Any soil   Sun or shade

IBERIS UMBELLATA CANDYTUFT
A common, easy to grow hardy annual for bedding out in the summer. The clusters of fragrant white, pink or ruby flowers appear from May to August and provide nectar for many insects including butterflies, particularly the meadow brown, small tortoiseshell and gatekeeper.

0.3 × 0.3   Any well-drained soil   Sun

Hesperis matronalis

Iberis   *Iris pseudacorus*

ILEX AQUIFOLIUM COMMON HOLLY

Common holly is one of our few native evergreen trees, growing as a hedgerow plant or woodland undershrub throughout the British Isles. Specimens are either male or female. Both bear pretty white nectar-rich flowers in May which attract insects including bees. The female flowers then develop into berries that are eaten by birds, especially thrushes. The prickly leaves and dense branching of a hedgerow holly make it an ideal nesting site. Holly also means food to the caterpillars of the holly blue butterfly.

5.0 × 3.0   Any soil   Sun or shade

IRIS PSEUDACORUS YELLOW IRIS

A native perennial of freshwater margins with yellow flags from June to August. A must for the edge of a wildlife pond or bog garden – providing shelter for amphibians and shade

Lavandula angustifolia 'Hidcote'

for other pond life. As with many plants pollinated by insects, the flowers are designed as honey-guides and include a suitable landing platform – even for the heavy bumble-bee.

0.8 × 0.4   Very moist or water's edge   Sun or part shade

LAVANDULA LAVENDER

A favourite evergreen or semi-evergreen sub-shrub in British gardens for many centuries. The grey or grey-green foliage is topped by pink, white, but principally blue flowers between July and September. Both the leaves and the blooms are scented. All manner of insects find lavender irresistible, and it is hard to beat for attracting a wide range of butterflies. Being a compact plant – especially the dwarf varieties such as 'Hidcote' and 'Munstead' – lavender is suitable for even the smallest wildlife plot.

0.3 to 0.6 × 0.4   Well-drained soil   Sun or a little shade

Limnanthes douglasii

LIGUSTRUM PRIVET
Privet are extremely adaptable evergreen or semi-evergreen shrubs. *L. vulgare* is a British native that provides food for the privet hawk-moth caterpillars and black berries for birds in the autumn. *L. ovalifolium* makes a better hedging or flowering plant. The white flower spikes come through in May and the strong, sickly scent invites masses of insects to drink the nectar. The more decorative gold and variegated varieties of *L. ovalifolium* do the same wildlife job.

2.0 × 1.5   Any soil   Any site

LIMNANTHES DOUGLASII POACHED EGG FLOWER
This unusual hardy annual makes a refreshing change to the lobelia and white alyssum in summer hanging baskets, tubs or at the front of borders. The common name describes the two-tone flowers – white with a yellow centre. Flowers

appear all summer and although visited by butterflies and other insects, bees can not get enough of them. Sow seeds in March where they are to flower.

0.15 × 0.2   Any soil   Sunny site

LONICERA PERICLYMENUM   HONEYSUCKLE OR WOODBINE

This native climber or scrambler will clamber over fences and arches or through trees and hedges. It produces masses of red, purple and cream tubular flowers from June to August which emit a powerful scent, especially in the evenings when they are visited by a number of moths, including the convolvulus and pine hawk-moths. During the day, the nectar-rich flowers supply other insects, but only those with tongues long enough to reach down the long tubes. The leaves are the food of the larvae of the rare white admiral butterfly. In autumn, the red juicy berries are devoured by birds. The untidy, twisting branch systems of mature specimens are often used for nesting by small birds. Planting two improved varieties – 'Belgica' (May and June) and 'Serotina' (July to October) – prolongs the flowering season.

4.0 × 2.0   Fertile loam   Sun or part shade

LUNARIA ANNUA   HONESTY

A beautiful hardy biennial much loved by flower arrangers for the flat moon-like seed pods. In late spring and early summer the small purple or white flowers appear above broad, toothed leaves. Larvae of the orange tip butterfly will feed on honesty and many insects enjoy the nectar contained within the flowers. It readily seeds itself around giving an informal style to your wildlife garden.

0.9 × 0.4   Well-drained soil   Sun or shade

LYCHNIS FLOS-CUCULI   RAGGED ROBIN

One of hundreds of native perennials ideal for planting in a

Lonicera periclymenum

Lunaria annua seed

Lychnis flos-cuculi

Lythrum salicarlica 'Robert'

Malus floribunda

wildlife meadow or lawn (see Checklist). The deeply cut, purplish-pink flowers are immediately recognizable and appear from May to August. Many insects including butterflies and bees visit the flowers. Ragged Robin will also grow under trees as long as it is not too dry.

0.35 × 0.3   Damp soils   Sun or shade

LYTHRUM SALICARLICA   PURPLE LOOSESTRIFE
A stout native perennial with whorls of reddish-purple flowers – which attract butterflies and bees – forming tall spikes from June to August. It prefers a damp site but will grow equally well in a humus-rich border. Excellent for marshy areas around a wildlife pond.

1.5 × 0.5   Any moisture-retentive soil   Sun or part shade

MALUS   CRAB APPLE
Deciduous trees of which the truly wild species (*M. sylvestris*) is rare in cultivation. Fortunately, there are many decorative

Muscari armeniacum 'Blue Spike'

varieties and hybrids which flower and fruit well. Many birds will nest among the congested branches and eat the variously sized and coloured fruits – except those that are yellow – in autumn. The flowers are pollinated by a number of insects, especially bees. Popular small fruiting varieties suitable for even quite small gardens include *M.* 'John Downie', *M.* 'Van Eseltine' and, for flowers, *M. floribunda* or *M.* 'Profusion'.

6.0 × 5.0   Any but boggy   Sun or part shade

MUSCARI GRAPE HYACINTH
A useful clump-forming bulbous plant producing principally blue flower spikes in April and May. Suitable for rock gardens, the front of borders, under trees in dappled shade or spring wildflower lawns where it will self-seed.

0.25 × 0.2   Well-drained soil   Sun or part shade

MYOSOTIS FORGET-ME-NOT
A hardy biennial much grown and loved for its tiny blue or

pink flowers in April and May. Hybrids of *M. alpestris* and *M. sylvatica* are the types often used in spring bedding schemes, but in a wildlife garden allow it to seed itself around. Suitable for mini-habitats, the flowers are visited by insects, especially bees. The water forget-me-not (*M. scorpioides*) is a British native suitable for wildlife pond edges.

0.15 to 0.35 × 0.3 to 0.45   Well-drained   Sun or part shade

MYRIOPHYLLUM × SPICATUM SPIKED WATER MILFOIL
Aquatic perennial with brown feathery foliage producing erect spikes of inconspicuous flowers above the water-line in early summer. The rest of the plant remains under water and is an important oxygenating plant for the wildlife pond. A bit rampant for small areas of water but provides plenty of shade and cover for pond life.

0.2 × 1.0   Fresh water   Sunny position

NICOTIANA ALATA TOBACCO PLANT
N. alata is a half-hardy annual bedding plant with white, green or various shades of red-flowered forms which are produced from June to the first frosts. The straight species in particular produces an enveloping evening scent, appreciated both by humans and by night-flying insects to which it signals a rich source of nectar.

0.2 × 0.4   Well-drained soil   Sun or shade

NYMPHAEA × HELVOLA WATER-LILY
There are hundreds of water-lilies, many of them too rampant for small ponds and considered too 'cultivated' in appearance for truly wild ponds. Water lilies do however have a role to play for pond wildlife – they provide plenty of shade and cover for water insects and other aquatic life as well as sunbathing and fly-catching platforms for frogs. *N. × helvola* is a good compromise. This hybrid is a dwarf with soft yellow flowers – not at all gaudy like some. For large ponds or even

Myosotis

Nicotiana

Nymphaea

Origanum vulgare 'Aureum'

lakes, choose *N. alba*, the native species with white flowers or some of the varieties of *N. × marliacea*. For miniature ponds – for example in half oak barrels – choose *N. tetragona*.

0.15 × 0.5   Freshwater   Sun

....

OLEARIA   DAISY BUSH
A genus of evergreen, wind-resistant shrubs native to Australasia. All have daisy-like flower heads, which are usually white and appear in late spring or summer. Some species make dense shrubs, such as *O. × haastii* and *O. × macrodonta*, which make good shelter or hedging plants, particularly for coastal gardens. The flowers are constantly visited by insects, including bees and butterflies.

2.0 × 1.5   Well-drained soil, especially chalk   Exposed, sun or
part shade

....

ORIGANUM VULGARE   MARJORAM
Many herbs attract pollinating insects when in flower.

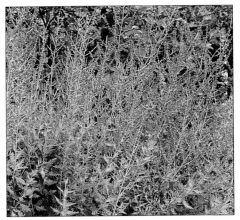

Perovskia atriplicifolia

Marjoram is a good example of a wildlife garden plant which also has culinary uses. The straight species is a native of dry, rough grassland and shrubby banks and so will tolerate growing in gravel or between paving slabs. There are various varieties, mainly with gold colouration to the leaves.

0.5 × 0.5   Well-drained soil, especially chalk   Sun

PEROVSKIA ATRIPLICIFOLIA RUSSIAN SAGE
A very attractive sub-shrub that at first glance looks like a giant lavender, especially when the blue flower spikes are produced in late summer. The whole plant is aromatic and is pollinated by bees.

1.2 × 1.0   Well-drained   Sun

PRIMULA DENTICULATA DRUMSTICK PRIMROSE
An attractive perennial with mauve, white or ruby-coloured flowers arranged in a globular head (hence the common

name) in March to April. It grows well in moist areas near the edge of a pond in a cool location. Many other primulas grow well in this type of position. The native species such as the primrose (*P. vulgaris*) and the oxlip (*P. elatior*) will colonise moist shady areas, grassy meadows or spring wild flower lawns, especially on heavy soils. For drier conditions try naturalizing the native cowslip (*P. veris*). All are a nectar source for insects.

0.1 to 0.2 × 0.1   Moist soil   Sun or shade

PYRACANTHA FIRETHORN
Evergreen, spiny shrubs usually preferring the support of a wall. The small white flowers in June are visited by insects but the main attraction to wildlife is in autumn when the red, orange or yellow berries are a favourite food of birds. The compact branch habit also provides a good nesting site.

4.0 × 3.0   Any soil   Sun or shade

QUERCUS ROBUR PEDUNCULATE OAK
This is the most common of our native oak trees. A large long-lived deciduous tree of woods, commons, pastures and hedgerows. Obviously too large for most gardens but over 400 different species of insects call it home as well as numerous birds and mammals – so one specimen nearby is of great benefit to a wildlife garden.

35.0 × 25.0   Any well-drained soil   Any site

RHAMNUS FRANGULA ALDER BUCKTHORN
A deciduous native shrub or small tree seldom noticed in the countryside. The small green flowers are inconspicuous but the reddish fruits that turn black when ripe are decorative for a short while, before being devoured by birds. With the purging buckthorn (*R. catharticus*) it is the main food plant of the larvae of the yellow brimstone butterfly.

5.0 × 3.0   Any soil, but prefers moist and acid   Sun or shade

Primula denticulata

Pyracantha

Rosa canina

ROSA ROSE
There are about 100 species of wild roses throughout the world and, of course, many thousands of cultivated varieties and hybrids. All will attract aphids and other plant pests, which means food for ladybirds and other predators, but perhaps the wild species native of Britain and Europe are most appropriate for a wildlife garden. *Rosa canina* is the dog rose with pink or white flowers in June, followed by red hips in autumn, which are eaten by many birds. Other native species include the field rose (*R. arvensis*) and the burnet rose (*R. pimpinellifolia*), which tolerates very dry conditions.

3.0 × 2.0   Any soil   Sun or part shade

SALIX WILLOW
A large group of deciduous trees or shrubs that includes a number native to Britain. Even small wildlife gardens can include a willow because they can be contained by hard pruning (stooling) every spring. They are thirsty plants so avoid planting near to buildings on a heavy clay soil. Willows support a wide range of wildlife (over 250 species of insect). The early catkin flowers are of great value to bees and the leaves are food for butterfly and moth larvae.

3.0 to 15.0 × 3.0 to 8.0   Any soil, especially moist   Any site

Scabiosa arvensis (Knautia arvensis)

SCABIOSA SCABIOUS

Perennial border plants (*S. caucasica*) that, when in flower attract a wide variety of insects. Flowers are mainly blue but white and pink forms exist. *S.* 'Butterfly Blue' is especially long-flowering (May to October) and attractive to butterflies. Many of the wild species such as *S. columbaria* and the field scabious (confusingly in another genus – *Knautia*) are recommended for wild flower lawns and meadows. The annual sweet scabious (*S. atropurpurea*) is particularly attractive to butterflies.

0.6 × 0.3   Well-drained, chalk preferred   Sun

SEDUM SPECTABILE STONECROP, ICE PLANT

A popular herbaceous perennial with plates of pink or red flowers from August to October. Probably the best perennial for attracting butterflies. It is not unusual to see over 20 on just one little plant. Ideal for the front of a nectar border.

0.45 × 0.4   Well-drained soil   Full sun

SOLIDAGO GOLDENROD
Herbaceous perennials that will attract insects when the yellow flowers are open from July to September. *S. virgaurea*, a native species, is especially good, but there are many attractive garden hybrid forms that can be used.

0.6 × 0.4   Well-drained soil   Sun or light shade

SORBUS AUCUPARIA MOUNTAIN ASH, ROWAN
A small native tree suitable for medium-sized wildlife gardens. Creamy white flowers in May to June, followed by scarlet berries in autumn. The flowers are visited by insects and the berries much sought after by many birds, particularly thrushes.

15.0 × 5.0   Any soil except heavy clay   Sun or shade

THYMUS THYME
Small woody herbs, some species of which are natives. Aromatic leaves and small pink, white or red flowers in June to July. Used in containers, rock gardens, or in the gaps between paving; some species will grow well in dry wildflower lawns. The flowers are pollinated by insects, especially bees.

0.3 × 0.4   Well drained soil   Full sun

VIBURNUM
A large group of evergreen and deciduous shrubs of varying stature. Many of the evergreen varieties, such as *V. tinus*, make suitable plants for shelter and bird nesting. *V.* × *bodnantense* and *V. farreri* flower in winter and early spring and can be life-savers to newly-emerging insects. There are two natives, the guelder rose (*V. opulus*) and the wayfaring tree (*V. lantana*), which both produce berries eaten by birds.

1.0 to 4.0 × 1.0 to 3.0   Good loam – acid or chalk   Sun or part shade

All the plants in the Directory are decorative to varying degrees and of use in a wildlife garden. Obviously, many plants that we term 'weeds' are also useful to wildlife (see Checklists).

Sedum spectabile

Solidago

Sorbus aucuparia

Thymus

Viburnum opulus

PLANT CHECKLISTS

A FINGERTIP GUIDE TO PLANTS FOR A WILDLIFE GARDEN

A wild flower garden and pond with cowslips, irises and foxgloves

PLANTS FOR THE WILDLIFE WATER AND BOG GARDEN

Ajuga reptans Bugle B
Angelica sylvestris Angelica MB
Butomus umbellatus Flowering Rush M
Callitriche stagnalis Water Starwort O
Caltha palustris Marsh Marigold MB
Cardamine pratensis Lady's Smock MB
Carex Sedge MB

Ceratophyllum demersum Hornwort FO
Cornus alba Red-barked Dogwood S
Cyperus longus Galingale M
Epilobium hirsutum Greater Willowherb B
Eupatorium cannabinum Hemp Agrimony B
Filipendula ulmaria Meadowsweet B
Fritillaria meleagris Snake's-head Fritillary B
Geum rivale Water Avens B

Hottonia palustris Water Violet F
Hydrocharis morsus-ranae Frogbit F
Iris pseudacorus Yellow Iris MB
Luronium natans Floating Water-plaintain F
Lychnis flos-cuculi Ragged Robin B
Lycopus europaeus Gipsywort M
Lysimachia nemorum Wood Pimpernel B
Lysimachia vulgaris Yellow Loosestrife M
Lythrum salicaria Purple Loosestrife MB
Mentha aquatica Water Mint M
Menyanthes trifoliata Bogbean M
Mimulus guttatus Monkeyflower (invasive) M
Myosotis scorpioides Water Forget-me-not MB
Myriophyllum spicatum Spiked Water-milfoil O
Nymphaea Water-lily F
Nymphoides peltata Fringed Water-lily or Buckbean F
Osmunda regalis Royal Fern B
Persicaria amphibia Amphibious Bistort M
Primula Candelabra types B
Ranunculus lingua Greater Spearwort M
Ranunculus Water-crowfoot F
Sagittaria sagittifolia Arrowhead M
Salix Willow S
Typha Reedmace M
Veronica beccabunga Brooklime M
Viburnum opulus Guelder Rose S

Key

M – Marginal plants for the pond edge, in shallow water
F – Floating plants
O – Oxygenating plants (usually submerged or partially submerged)
B – Bog plants for wet soils
S – Shrubs for the water's edge

PLANTS FOR WOODLAND, WOODLAND EDGE AND SHADE

Aconitum napellus Monkshood
Ajuga reptans Bugle
Anemone nemorosa Wood Anemone
Aquilegia vulgaris Columbine
Arum maculatum Lords-and-Ladies
Convallaria majalis Lily-of-the-Valley
Digitalis purpurea Foxglove
Euphorbia amygdaloides Wood Spurge
Filipendula ulmaria Meadowsweet
Galium odoratum Woodruff
Geum rivale Water Avens
Geum urbanum Wood Avens
Glechoma hederacea Ground Ivy
Hedera helix Ivy
Helleborus Christmas and Lenten Rose
Hesperis matronalis Dame's Violet
Hyacinthoides non-scripta Bluebell
Iris foetidissima Stinking Iris
Lamiastrum galeobdolon Yellow Archangel
Lonicera periclymenum Honeysuckle
Luzula sylvatica Great Woodrush
Melica uniflora Wood Millet
Narcissus pseudonarcissus Wild Daffodil
Polygonatum multiflorum Solomon's Seal
Primula vulgaris Primrose
Ruscus aculeatus Butcher's Broom
Teucrium scorodonia Wood Sage
Vicia sylvatica Wood Vetch
Viola odorata Sweet Violet

Fritillaria meleagris

WILDFLOWERS FOR LAWNS AND MEADOWS

Achillea millefolium Yarrow
Agrimonia eupatoria Agrimony
Agrostemma githago Corncockle
Ajuga reptans Bugle
Anthyllis vulneraria Kidney Vetch
Bellis perennis Daisy
Caltha palustris Marsh Marigold
Campanula rotundifolia Harebell
Cardamine pratensis Lady's Smock
Centaurea cyanus Cornflower
Centaurea nigra Common Knapweed
Centaurea scabiosa Greater Knapweed
Chrysanthemum segetum Corn Marigold
Clinopodium vulgare Wild Basil
Colchicum autumnale Meadow Saffron
Filipendula ulmaria Meadowsweet
Fritillaria meleagris Snake's-head Fritillary

Galanthus nivalis Snowdrop
Galium verum Lady's Bedstraw
Geranium pratense Meadow Crane's-bill
Hesperis matronalis Dame's Violet
Hippocrepis comosa Horseshoe Vetch
Hyacinthoides non-scripta Bluebell
Hypericum perforatum Perforate St John's-wort
Hypochoeris radicata Cat's-ear
Knautia arvensis Field Scabious
Lathyrus pratensis Meadow Vetchling
Leontodon autumnalis Autumn Hawkbit
Leontodon hispidus Rough Hawkbit
Leucanthemum vulgare Ox-eye Daisy
Lotus corniculatus Bird's-foot Trefoil
Lotus uliginosa Greater bird's-foot Trefoil
Lychnis flos-cuculi Ragged Robin
Medicago lupulina Black Medick
Muscari Grape Hyacinth
Narcissus pseudonarcissus Wild Daffodil
Ononis repens Common Restharrow
Origanum vulgare Marjoram
Ornithogalum umbellatum Star-of-Bethlehem
Papaver rhoeas Corn Poppy
Pilosella officinarum Mouse-ear Hawkweed
Plantago lanceolata Ribwort Plantain
Plantago media Hoary Plantain
Potentilla erecta Tormentil
Primula veris Cowslip
Prunella vulgaris Self-heal
Ranunculus acris Meadow Buttercup

Ranunculus bulbosus Bulbous Buttercup
Ranunculus ficaria Lesser Celandine
Rhinanthus minor Yellow Rattle
Rumex acetosa Common Sorrel
Sanguisorba minor Salad Burnet
Sanguisorba officinalis Greater Burnet
Saponaria officinalis Soapwort
Saxifraga granulata Meadow Saxifrage
Scabiosa columbaria Small Scabious
Silene alba White Campion
Silene dioica Red Campion
Stellaria graminea Lesser Stitchwort
Taraxacum officinale Dandelion
Thymus Thyme
Tragopogon pratensis Goat's-beard
Trifolium dubium Lesser Trefoil
Trifolium pratense Red Clover
Veronica chamaedrys Germander Speedwell
Veronica filiformis Slender Speedwell
Vicia cracca Tufted Vetch

ATTRACTIVE AND/OR USEFUL 'WEEDS' FOR THE WILDLIFE GARDEN

Achillea millefolium Yarrow
Anthriscus sylvestris Cow Parsley
Bellis perennis Daisy
Chelidonium majus Greater Celandine
Circaea lutetiana Enchanter's Nightshade
Geranium robertianum Herb Robert
Glechoma hederacea Ground Ivy
Papaver rhoeas Corn Poppy

Petasites fragrans Winter Heliotrope
Rumex Sorrel
Taraxacum officinale Dandelion
Urtica dioica Stinging Nettle
Veronica filiformis Slender Speedwell

PLANTS FOR HEDGEROW/ NESTING PURPOSES

Berberis Barberry
Ceanothus Californian Lilac
Chamaecyparis lawsoniana Lawson Cypress
Cornus alba Red-barked dogwood
Cornus sanguinea Dogwood★
Cotoneaster
Crataegus monogyna Hawthorn★
Escallonia
Hedera helix Ivy
Ilex aquifolium Holly
Ligustrum ovalifolium Oval-leaved Privet
Ligustrum vulgare Common Privet
Lonicera periclymenum Honeysuckle★
Malus Apple, Crab Apple
Olearia Daisy Bush
Pyracantha Firethorn
Quercus Oak★
Rosa arvensis Field Rose★
Rosa canina Dog Rose★
Salix Willow★
Viburnum lantana Wayfaring Tree★
Viburnum opulus Guelder Rose★
Viburnum tinus Laurustinus

★British native plants (see also Native Trees and Shrubs Checklists – many are suitable under this category)

PLANTS THAT PROVIDE FOOD FOR WILD BIRDS (SEEDS AND BERRIES)

Anthriscus sylvestris Cow Parsley
Antirrhinum Snapdragon
Arctium Burdock
Aronia arbutifolia Red Chokeberry
Aster Michaelmas Daisy
Berberis Barberry
Callistephus China Aster
Centaurea Knapweed
Cirsium, Carduus, Onopordon etc Thistle
Cornus sanguinea Dogwood
Cotoneaster
Crataegus monogyna Hawthorn
Dipsacus sylvestris Teasel
Erysimum Wallflower
Euonymus europaeus Spindle Bush
Filipendula ulmaria Meadowsweet
Fragaria Strawberry
Hedera helix Ivy
Helianthus annuus Sunflower
Heracleum Hogweed
Ilex aquifolium Holly
Ligustrum vulgare Privet
Lonicera periclymenum and others Honeysuckle

Malus sylvestris and varieties Crab Apple
Oenothera biennis Evening Primrose
Plantago Plantain
Prunus padus Bird Cherry
Pyracantha Firethorn
Rosa canina Dog Rose
Rubus fruticosus and others Brambles, Blackberries
Sambucus nigra Elder
Senecio vulgare Groundsel
Sorbus aucuparia Mountain Ash
Stellaria media Chickweed
Taraxacum officinale Dandelion
Taxus baccata Yew
Urtica dioica Stinging Nettle
Viburnum lantana Wayfaring Tree
Viburnum opulus Guelder Rose

NECTAR PLANTS FOR INSECTS

Agrimonia eupatoria Agrimony
Agrostemma githago Corncockle
Alyssum Alyssum
Amelanchier Snowy Mespilus
Aster Michaelmas Daisy
Aubrieta
Buddleja Butterfly bush
Calendula Marigold
Calluna vulgaris Heather or Ling
Cardamine pratensis Lady's Smock
Caryopteris × *clandonensis* Shrubby Verbena
Ceanothus Californian Lilac
Centaurea Cornflower, Knapweed
Centranthus ruber Red Valerian
Ceratostigma Hardy Plumbago
Cistus Sun Rose
Cornus Dogwood
Crataegus monogyna Hawthorn
Dahlia

Daphne odora Daphne
Dianthus barbatus Sweet William
Dipsacus sylvestris Teasel
Echinops ritro Globe Thistle
Erica carnea Heather
Erysimum cheiri Wallflower
Escallonia
Hebe Shrubby Veronica
Hedera helix Ivy
Heliotropium Heliotrope
Hesperis matronalis Dame's Violet
Hyssopus officinalis Hyssop
Iberis Candytuft
Ilex aquifolium Holly
Iris pseudacorus Yellow Iris
Knautia Scabious
Lavandula Lavender
Ligustrum Privet
Limnanthus douglasii Poached-egg
  Plant
Lonicera periclymenum
  Honeysuckle
Lychnis flos-cuculi Ragged Robin
Lythrum salicaria Purple
  Loosestrife
Malus Apple
Mentha Mint
Myosotis Forget-me-not
Nicotiana Tobacco Plant

Olearia Daisy Bush
Onobrychis viciifolia Sainfoin
Origanum Marjoram
Perovskia atriplicifolia Russian Sage
Phuopsis stylosa Phuopsis
Primula Cowslip, Oxslip,
  Primrose etc.
Prunus padus Bird Cherry
Prunus spinosus Sloe
Pulicaria dysenterica Fleabane
Pyracantha Firethorn
Pyrus communis Wild Pear
Reseda odorata Mignonette
Rubus fruticosus Bramble,
  Blackberry
Rubus idaeus Raspberry
Salix Willow
Saponaria officinalis Soapwort
Scabiosa Scabious
Sedum Stonecrop, Iceplant
Serratula tinctoria Saw-wort
Solidago Goldenrod
Spiraea
Syringa Lilac
Thymus Thyme
Tussilago farfara Coltsfoot
Verbena
Viburnum tinus Laurustinus
Viburnum × bodnantense Viburnum

FOODPLANTS FOR CATERPILLARS (MOTHS AND BUTTERFLIES)

Plant	*Moth/butterfly*
Angelica sylvestris Angelica	Swallowtail
Arabis Rock Cress	Orange Tip
Arctium Burdock	Painted Lady
Calendula Marigold	Chalk Hill Blue
Cardamine pratensis Lady's Smock	Orange Tip, Green Veined White
Chamerion angustifolium Rosebay Willowherb	Elephant Hawk-moth
Clarkia elegans Clarkia	Elephant Hawk-moth
Digitalis Foxglove	Heath Fritillary
Euonymus europaeus Spindle Bush	Holly Blue
Foeniculum Fennel	Swallowtail
Fragaria Strawberry	Grizzled Skipper, Green Hairstreak
Fraxinus Ash	Privet Hawk-moth
Fuchsia	Elephant Hawk-moth
Hedera Ivy	Holly Blue
Helianthemum Rock Rose	Green Hairstreak, Brown Argus
Hesperis matronalis Dame's Violet	Small Copper
Humulus lupulus Hop	Comma, Red Admiral
Ilex aquifolium Holly	Holly Blue
Ligustrum Privet	Privet Haw-kmoth
Lonicera periclymenum Honeysuckle	Marsh Fritillary, White Admiral
Lotus Birds-foot Trefoil	Pale Clouded Yellow, Common Blue, Dingy Skipper, Burnet Moth, Green Hairstreak, Short-tailed Blue, Silver-spotted Skipper
Lunaria annua Honesty	Orange Tip
Lupinus arboreus Tree Lupin	Long-Tailed Blue
Malus Apple	Eyed Hawk-moth
Origanum Marjoram	Scotch Argus, Chequered Skipper, Large Heath
Plantago Plantain	Marsh Fritillary, Glanville Fritillary, Heath Fritillary
Populus Poplar	Poplar Hawk-moth
Primula veris Cowslip	Duke of Burgundy Fritillary
Rhamnus catharticus Purging Buckthorn	Brimstone
Rhamnus frangula Alder Buckthorn	Brimstone

Viola cornuta

Ribes uva-crispa Gooseberry	Comma
Ribes Currant	Comma
Rubus Blackberry	Grizzled Skipper, Green Hairstreak
Rumex Sorrel	Small Copper
Rumex Dock	Small Copper
Salix Willow	Eyed Hawk-moth, Poplar Hawk-moth
Scabiosa Scabious	Marsh Fritillary
Syringa Lilac	Privet Hawk-moth
Teucrium scorodonia Wood Sage	Heath Fritillary
Thymus Thyme	Large Blue
Tilia Lime	Lime Hawk-moth
Trifolium Clover	Mazarine Blue, Short-tailed Blue, Clouded Yellow, Pale Clouded Yellow
Ulex Gorse	Short-tailed Blue, Long-tailed Blue, Green Hairstreak, Holly Blue
Urtica dioica Stinging Nettle	Red Admiral, Comma, Peacock, Small Tortoiseshell, Pale Clouded Yellow
Viola Violet	Silver Washed Fritillary, Pearl Bordered Fritillary, Dark Green Fritillary, High Brown Fritillary, Queen of Spain Fritillary
Viola Pansy	Pearl Bordered Fritillary, Queen of Spain Fritillary

Grasses, thistles, vetch and many members of the cabbage (Cruciferae) and pea (legume) families also provide food for a very wide range of butterfly and moth caterpillars.

NIGHT-SCENTED PLANTS THAT ATTRACT MOTHS

Centranthus ruber Red Valerian
Clematis vitalba Traveller's Joy★
Eschscholzia californica Californian
  Poppy
Hesperis matronalis Dame's Violet
Jasminum officinale Summer
  Jasmine
Lathyrus sylvestris Everlasting Pea★
Lonicera periclymenum
  Honeysuckle★
Matthiola longipetala subsp. *bicornis*
  Night-scented Stock
Nicotiana Tobacco Plant
Oenothera Evening Primrose
Petunia × *hybrida* Petunia
Phlox
Saponaria officinalis Soapwort
Silene alba White Campion
Silene noctiflora Night-scented
  Catchfly★
Silene vulgaris Bladder Campion★
Verbena

★British native plants

SMALL PLANTS SUITABLE FOR MINI-HABITATS, CONTAINERS OR SMALL WILDLIFE GARDENS

Alyssum Alyssum
Arabis Rock Cress
Aubrieta Aubrieta
Calluna vulgaris Heather or Ling
Convallaria majalis Lily of the
  Valley
Dianthus barbatus Sweet William
Erica carnea Heather
Fragaria vesca Wild Strawberry
Galanthus nivalis Snowdrop
Hedera helix Ivy (small-leaved
  varieties)
Hesperis matronalis Dame's Violet
Hyacinthoides non-scripta Bluebell
Lavandula Lavender
Limnanthes douglasii Poached-egg
  Plant
Lychnis flos-cuculi Ragged Robin
Muscari Grape Hyacinth
Mysotis Forget-me-not
Nicotiana Tobacco Plant
Nymphaea pygmaea Water-lily (for
  very small ponds)
Nymphaea × *helvola* Water-lily
  (for small ponds)
Origanum Marjoram
Primula Cowslip, Oxslip etc.
Thymus Thyme
Viola Violet and pansy

Additionally, most annual bedding
plants and wild flowers are small
enough to be included here.

NATIVE SHRUBS AND CLIMBERS

Calluna vulgaris Heather or Ling
Clematis vitalba Old Man's Beard or Traveller's Joy
Cornus sanguinea Dogwood
Corylus avellana Hazel
Cytisus scoparius Broom
Daphne laureola Spurge Laurel
Daphne mezereum Mezereon
Erica cinerea Bell Heather
Erica tetralix Cross-leaved Heath
Frangula alnus Alder Buckthorn
Hedera helix Ivy
Hippophaë rhamnoides Sea Buckthorn
Hypericum androsaemum Tutsan
Juniperus communis Juniper★
Ligustrum vulgare Wild Privet
Lonicera periclymenum Honeysuckle
Myrica gale Bog Myrtle
Prunus spinosa Sloe or Blackthorn
Rhamnus catharticus Purging Buckthorn
Rosa arvensis Field Rose
Rosa canina Dog Rose
Rubus fruticosus Bramble
Ruscus aculeatus Butcher's Broom
Salix cinerea Grey Willow
Salix purpurea Purple Willow
Salix viminalis Osier Willow
Sambucus nigra Elder
Ulex europaeus Gorse
Vaccinium myrtillus Bilberry
Viburnum lantana Wayfaring Tree
Viburnum opulus Guelder Rose

NATIVE TREES

Acer campestre Field Maple
Alnus glutinosa Alder
Betula pendula Silver Birch
Betula pubescens Downy Birch
Carpinus betulus Hornbeam
Crataegus laevigata Midland Hawthorn
Crataegus monogyna Hawthorn
Fagus sylvatica Beech
Fraxinus excelsior Ash
Ilex aquifolium Holly
Malus sylvestris sylvestris Crab Apple
Pinus sylvestris ssp Scots Pine★
Populus nigra var. *betulifolia* Black Poplar
Populus tremula Aspen
Prunus avium Wild Cherry or Gean
Prunus padus Bird Cherry
Pyrus communis Wild Pear
Quercus petraea Sessile Oak
Quercus robur Common or Pedunculate Oak
Salix alba White Willow
Salix caprea Goat Willow
Salix fragilis Crack Willow
Sorbus aria Whitebeam
Sorbus aucuparia Rowan or Mountain Ash
Sorbus torminalis Wild Service Tree
Taxus baccata Yew★
Tilia cordata Small-leaved Lime
Ulmus glabra Wych Elm

★Conifers

Useful organizations

The Bat Conservation Trust (see The Conservation Foundation)

British Hedgehog Preservation Society, Knowbury House, Knowbury, Ludlow, Shropshire

British Trust for Conservation Volunteers (BTCV), *London Office:* 80 York Way, London N1 9AG, *Head Office:* 36 St. Mary's Street, Wallingford, Oxfordshire OX10 0EH

British Trust for Ornithology (BTO), Beech Grove, Tring, Hertfordshire HP23 5NR

Butterfly Conservation, PO Box 222, Dedham, Colchester, Essex CO7 6EY

The Conservation Foundation, 1 Kensington Gore, London SW7 2AR

Countryside Council for Wales, Plas Penrhos, Fford, Penrhos, Bangor, Gwynedd LL57 2LQ

Henry Doubleday Research Association, Ryton Gardens, Ryton-on-Dunsmore, Coventry CV8 3LG

English Nature (formerly the Nature Conservancy Council), Northminster House, Peterborough PE1 1UA

Fauna and Flora Preservation Society (FFPS), Zoological Gardens, Regent's Park, London NW1 4RY

Field Studies Council, 62 Wilson Street, London EC2A 2BU

Friends of the Earth (FOE), 26-28 Underwood Street, London N1 7JQ

Mammal Society, Department of Zoology, Bristol University, Woodland Road, Bristol BS8 1UG

Nature Conservancy Council for Scotland, 12 Hope Terrace, Edinburgh EH9 2AS

Royal Society for Nature Conservation (RSNC), The Green, Nettleham, Lincolnshire LN2 2NR

Royal Society for the Protection of Birds (RSPB), The Lodge, Sandy, Bedfordshire SG19 2DL

Trust for Urban Ecology Ltd (TRUE), Ecological Gardens, Timberpond Road, London SE16 1AG

Young Ornithologists Club (YOC), The Lodge, Sandy , Bedfordshire SG19 2DL

Plant and seed suppliers

Most garden centres, plant centres and nurseries offer a wide range of suitable plants, but the following companies supply some of the more specialized types:

John Chambers, 15 Westleigh Road, Barton Seagrave, Kettering, Northamptonshire NN15 5AJ

Emorsgate Seed, Terrington Court, Terrington, St Clement, King's Lynn, Norfolk PE34 4NY

Kingsfield Conservation Nursery, Broadenham Lane, Winsham, Chard, Somerset TA20 4JF

Landlife Wildflowers Ltd (RPA), The Old Police Station, Lark Lane, Liverpool L17 8UU

Naturescape, Little Orchard, Main Street, Whatton in the Vale, Nottinghamshire NG13 9EP

Natural Selection, 1 Station Cottages, Hullavington, Chippenham, Wiltshire SN14 6ET

Picture Acknowledgements

b–bottom/c–centre/l–left/r–right/t–top
Heather Angel 33 (tr), 48
A–Z Botanical Collection 21
Eric Crichton 24 (cr), 30, 33 (br & cl), 35 (tl), 37, 39 (b), 40, 41,
43 (tr & b), 44, 51 (t, cr & bl), 52
Jerry Harpur front cover background, 11
Andrew Lawson 5, 23 (tl & b), 24 (tr & br), 26, 29 (t & b), 33 (tl & bl),
34, 35 (tr), 36, 39 (t), 45
S. & O. Mathews 47 (t), 49
Natural History Photographic Association/S. Dalton 15, 16, 19
Clive Nichols 24 (tl), 30, 43 (tl), 47 (b), 51 (cl & br), 54
Oxford Scientific Films front cover inset (S. Frithjof),
back cover (Photo Researchers, Inc.), 1 (G. A. Maclean),
9 (C. Milkins), 12 (H. Taylor), 56 (Photo Researchers, Inc.),
57 (S. Camazine), 60 (B. Watkins)
Photos Horticultural 24 (bl)
Harry Smith Collection 13, 23 (tl), 29 (cr)